Contending FOR THE FAITH

Veronica Chinasa Osunwa

A Note from the Publisher

The publisher wishes to acknowledge and thank Dr Douglas H. Johnson for his invaluable help and support for Africa World Books and its mission of preserving and promoting African cultural and literary traditions and history. Dr Johnson and fellow historians have been instrumental in ensuring that African people remain connected to their past and their identity. Africa World Books is proud to carry on this mission.

© *Chinasa Veronica Osunwa*, 2021

ISBN: 9780645363357

All rights reserved.

No part of this publication may be reproduced, stored in a retrieval system, or transmitted, in any form, or by any means, electronic, mechanical, photocopying, recording or otherwise, without the prior permission of the publishers.

This book is sold subject to the conditions that it shall not, by way of trade or otherwise, be lent, re-sold, hired out or otherwise circulated without the publisher's prior consent in any form of binding or cover other than in which it is published and without a similar condition including the condition being imposed on the subsequent purchaser.

Cover design, typesetting and layout : Africa World Books

Dear friends, although I was very eager to write to you about the salvation we share, I felt compelled to write and urge you to contend for the faith that was once for all entrusted to God's holy people
-Jude 3(NIV)

Forward

There is an increasingly popular self-deceiving worldview where truth has become whatever a person wants it to be. Where what "You" believe is "Truth" for you and what "I" believe is "Truth" for me. This lack of understanding of TRUTH is one of the key reasons behind the defeat of many Christians who fail in their Christian walk and end up shipwrecking their faith.

Jeremiah 6:16 counsels to "....ask for the old paths where the good way is and to walk in it then you will find rest for your souls". God is truth and the Knowledge of Jesus is the pathway to this truth.

In this book Veronica Chinasa Osunwa a battle proven God's general of the Faith from Perth Australia shows us the ancient paths by putting together into a cohesive framework the foundational truths upon which a victorious Christian Faith stands.

Leaping off from every page are the fundamental truths that are necessary for successful Christian living presented in a perfectly harmonious relationship that is understandable, interesting and relevant.

Contending for the Christian Faith has clarity and depth that provide answers to doctrinal questions such as the deity and personality of God as father, son and Holy Spirit. The mystery and necessity of the virgin birth. The blood of atonement. The wonder of the power in the name of Jesus and much more.

The book has laid out the facts that validate this truths in a simple but authoritative way that will strengthen the ability of the reader to live a full, rich, successful and victorious Christian Life

Anyone that wants to grow in understanding of the fundamentals truths that uphold the Christian Faith and have Faith in Jesus Christ. This book is for you. It will give you a deep understanding of Biblical foundational truth in an erudite and accessible way.

I highly and strongly recommend this book to the body of Christ.

Apostle Malcolm Orkar
Holy Spirit Ministries
Edinburgh, Scotland
United Kingdom.

Introduction

We live in a world of games, lies and deception and the truth are no longer seen as the truth. The lies and deceptions are being presented as the truth. If the truth must gain its place, there must be a fight for it.

Jesus is the way, the truth and the life and no man can come to the Father except by Him.

- *Jesus saith unto him, I am the way, the truth, and the life: no man cometh unto the Father, but by me.* **John 14:6**

A lot of doctrines and religion are undermining this truth and anything that does not point to Jesus is a way to destruction and death.

- *There is a way which seemeth right unto a man, but the end thereof are the ways of death.*
  Proverbs 14:12

As Christians who are privileged to know the truth, we must point people to the truth, the way, so that they can be saved. For us to successfully do this, we must contend for the faith. This means we must strive to surmount the challenges against our faith, we must continue to defend our belief and keep affirming against all odds that it is the "truth".

Our faith is what we hold sacred; it is our hope and trust for the supernatural. It is our complete trust and confidence in the one true God. This faith we are talking about is our strong belief in the doctrines of our religion based on spiritual conviction.

You may agree that, if this is what our faith is, then it is worth contending for. The fundamental Christian doctrines must be protected because it is the differentiating factor from other religions. It is these fundamentals that makes our faith genuine.

Christendom is controlled by faith. It is this faith itself that makes you accept Jesus as Lord. Everything you will ever do will have to be by faith. True faith in God must both accept and defend the fundamental Christian doctrines as revealed in the Bible.

- *But without faith it is impossible to please him…*

Hebrews 11:6a

This is what this book is about; to help you identify these fundamentals and teach you how to effectively contend for the faith in this light.

Chapter One
FUNDAMENTAL CHRISTIAN DOCTRINES AND TRUTHS

1. **The Deity and Personality of God as Triune, As Father, Son and Holy Spirit**

- *For there are three that bear record in heaven, the Father, the Word, and the Holy Ghost: and these three are one.* ***1 John 5:7***

You must belief in the doctrine of the trinity, which holds that God is one but with three co-eternal beings of God the Father, God the son: Jesus Christ and God the Holy Spirit. This is the central tenet of the Christian faith.

The Bible is clear on this matter and there are several bible passages to reinforce this fact. Other religions argue that we have three Gods, therefore, Christianity is a confused religion, but we know that we have but one God, manifesting in three ways.

This is what the Bible says, this is what the Christian faith believes and preaches, and this is what we must uphold as form of argument.

2. The Virgin Birth

People, especially those of the other religions, still argue the possibility of a virgin birth. The Christian doctrine believes in the virgin birth and takes what the Bible says concerning this as the truth. The virgin birth is one of the mysteries of the Christian faith. As a Christian or one who has faith in the true God, you must believe in this mystery.

Jesus could not have come into this world like every other ordinary human. He is God on a divine mission. There was need for his birth to be outstanding, unusual and extra-ordinary because He Himself is extra-ordinary.

- *Therefore the Lord himself shall give you a sign; Behold, a virgin shall conceive, and bear a son, and shall call his name Immanuel.* ***Isaiah 7:14***

The conception of a virgin was a sure sign promised by God to His people, so as to identify the saviour. In spite of the prophecy and fulfilment His own could not recognize Him.

- *Behold, a virgin shall be with child, and shall bring forth a son, and they shall call his name Emmanuel, which being interpreted is, God with us. Matthew 1:23*

In spite of the prophecy and fulfilment, His own could not recognize Him and some still don't recognize Him today. If Jesus were conceived naturally He could have been an ordinary man

3. The Blood of Jesus or the Blood of Atonement.

The blood of Jesus is the soul of the Christian faith. It is the essence of Christianity. There was nothing like Christianity until after Jesus shed His blood. The blood of Jesus is not a fiction; but the physical blood actually shed by Jesus Christ on the cross of Calvary and the salvation which Christianity teaches and preaches is accomplished through this. And this is why the argument or difference between Christianity and some other religions is the New Testament; which is the coming of Jesus Christ.

The blood of Jesus is our redemption; we are redeemed only because Jesus shed his blood for us.

18. *Forasmuch as ye know that ye were not redeemed with corruptible things, as silver and gold, from your vain conversation received by tradition from your fathers;*

19. *But with the precious blood of Christ, as of a lamb without blemish and without spot*

1 Peter 1:18-19

- *In whom we have redemption through his blood, the forgiveness of sins, according to the riches of his grace;* ***Ephesians 1:7***

Our sins are forgiven only because of the blood of Jesus.

The blood of Jesus gives us access to the presence of God.

- *But now in Christ Jesus ye who sometimes were far off are made nigh by the blood of Christ.* ***Ephesians 2:13***

19. Having therefore, brethren, boldness to enter into the holiest by the blood of Jesus,

20. By a new and living way, which he hath consecrated for us, through the veil, that is to say, his flesh;

21. And having an high priest over the house of God;

22. Let us draw near with a true heart in full assurance of faith, having our hearts sprinkled from an evil conscience, and our bodies washed with pure water. **Hebrews 10:19-22**

We are justified by the blood of Jesus.

- *Much more then, being now justified by his blood, we shall be saved from wrath through him.* **Romans 5:9**

Jesus already took our place and punishment and as a result made us guiltless.

4. The Name of Jesus.

The Name of Jesus, means Saviour. It is given to our Lord because "He saves His people from their Sin" He saves them from the guilt of sin by cleaning them in His own blood. When you hear the name Jesus or call the name Jesus, you are simply saying, the one whom saves. No wonder scripture says;

- *The name of the LORD is a strong tower: the righteous runneth into it, and is safe.* **Proverbs 18:10**

The name "Jesus" has been given to us by God the Father for our profiting. All things are possible in the name. The name of Jesus is sweet and precious to children of God. It does what money cannot do. It gives us inner peace and heals the troubled hearts.

The name of Jesus is above all names. Do not allow anyone cajole you to believe in anything or name other than the name Jesus.

After the name of Jesus, there is no other. That's what it means to be above all names.

- *Wherefore God also hath highly exalted him, and given him a name which is above every name:* **Philippians 2:9**

Jesus expects you to use the power and authority in his name. This power and authority rightfully belongs to a born-again Christian.

18. *And Jesus came and spake unto them, saying, All power is given unto me in heaven and in earth.*

19. *Go ye therefore, and teach all nations, baptizing them in the name of the Father, and of the Son, and of the Holy Ghost:*

20. *Teaching them to observe all things whatsoever I have commanded you: and, lo, I am with you always, even unto the end of the world. Amen.* **Matthew 28:18-20**

- *Behold, I give unto you power to tread on serpents and scorpions, and over all the power of the enemy: and nothing shall by any means hurt you.* **Luke 10:19**

- *But as many as received him, to them gave the power to become the sons of God, even to them that believe on his name:* **John 1:12**

You as a born again Christian have been delegated to use this power and authority because you believe in His name.

- *And these signs shall follow them that believe; In my name shall they cast out devils; they shall speak with new tongues;* **Mark 16:17**

There is a vast force in the power of the name of Jesus that it triumphs over any problem, any trial or situation. Demons flee from it and expire at its mention. Darkness is instantly shattered and even death cannot contend with the name of Jesus.

The name of Jesus is the entrance point and stamp of everything done in the Christian faith. You can put the name to work in every aspect of your life. The name of Jesus should always be your first resort and not your last resort. No other name carries the weight, power and efficiency this name Jesus carries. The name of Jesus offers supernatural protection; call it as your emergency number and it will come to you as a rescue vehicle.

5. The Second Coming

19. If in this life only we have hope in Christ, we are of all men most miserable.

20. But now is Christ risen from the dead, and become the first fruits of them that slept.

21. For since by man came death, by man came also the resurrection of the dead.

22. For as in Adam all die, even so in Christ shall all be made alive.

23. But every man in his own order: Christ the first fruits; afterward they that are Christ's at his coming. ***1 Corinthians 15:19-23***

The Christian faith is hinged on the second coming of Jesus Christ. This is the hope of the Christian and this is the whole essence of His birth, death and resurrection. The plan of salvation is in place to secure the children of God for eternity. If it were not so, then the Christian faith would be another call to misery.

There is life after death and salvation is meant to save us from the judgment of condemnation when Jesus comes. If there was no judgment or second coming as we see in the scripture above, then there will be absolutely no need for salvation. God does not want His creation to be condemned, hence He put a plan in place to save mankind;

- *For God so loved the world, that he gave his only begotten Son, that whosoever believeth in him should not perish, but have everlasting life. **John 3:16.***

Some other religions believe in the second coming too, but the difference is that Jesus is the plan of salvation for mankind as we see in scriptures and Jesus is the way, the truth and the life. No one would see God at death unless they embrace Him according to John 14:6. There is no other way to inherit eternal life; do not be deceived.

Beloved, these are the fundamentals of the Christian faith. These doctrines and truths are the central force of the Christian faith that we must contend for. These are the truths that the devil does not want a lot of people to believe or embrace. Even some of those who already believed and have embraced these truths are becoming double minded about these truths, which is why it is most pressing that we rise up and contend for the faith.

After Jesus, the Apostles contended for the faith and handed it down to others, who contended and handed it down, and so on until the gospel is now in our hands today. It is also our duty to contend for the faith to ensure that those doctrines and truths are not tainted and that we hand this on to generations after us.

There are arguments about the trinity, arguments that a man cannot die for another, arguments about the impossibility of the virgin birth and arguments about Jesus being an ordinary prophet like others. It is our duty to continually assert that what the Bible says about these mysteries is the truth because we are privileged to know the truth.

11. *And he said unto them, Unto you it is given to know the mystery of the kingdom of God: but unto them that are without, all these things are done in parables:*

12. *That seeing they may see, and not perceive; and hearing they may hear, and not understand; lest at any time they should be converted, and their sins should be forgiven them.* **Mark 4:11-12**

We must contend for the faith because there are many contrary doctrines out there hiding under the guise of the Christian faith. The Christian faith is under attack both from without and within, so we must contend to keep the faith handed down to us as it is.

- *For there are certain men crept in unawares, who were before of old ordained to this condemnation, ungodly men, turning the* *grace of our God into lasciviousness, and denying the only Lord God, and our Lord Jesus Christ. **Jude 1:4***

14. *But I have a few things against thee, because thou hast there them that hold the doctrine of Balaam, who taught Balac to cast a stumbling block before the children of Israel, to eat things sacrificed unto idols, and to commit fornication.*

15. *So hast thou also them that hold the doctrine of the Nicolaitans, which thing I hate.* **Revelation 2:14-15**

Child of God, you must defend the Christian faith.

Chapter Two
WHY SHOULD I CONTEND FOR THE CHRISTIAN FAITH?

1. **You Are an Ambassador of Christ.**

- *Now then we are ambassadors for Christ, as though God did beseech you by us: we pray you in Christ's stead, be ye reconciled to God.*
  2 Corinthians 5:20

This scripture makes it clear that you are Christ's representative. You are an important official, a high ranking diplomat accredited to represent Jesus and His kingdom and to reconcile men to Him.

Jesus has contended and won the battle; He is counting on you for His purpose to be fulfilled in the lives of others.

- *To wit, that God was in Christ, reconciling the world unto himself, not imputing their trespasses unto them; and hath committed* unto us the word of reconciliation.

2 Corinthians 5:19.

Contend for the faith by living a life worthy of an ambassador of God's kingdom.

- *Therefore be imitators of God as dear children.* **Ephesians 5:1.**

Represent and communicate the mind of God to this world as a representative of His kingdom. You must contend because you are an ambassador.

2. There are False Prophets and False Doctrines

- *And many false prophets shall rise, and shall deceive many.* **Matthew 24:11.**

- *For false Christs and false prophets shall rise, and shall shew signs and wonders, to seduce, if it were possible, even the elect.* **Mark 13:22.**

13. *For such are false apostles, deceitful workers, transforming themselves into the apostles of Christ.*

14. *And no marvel; for Satan himself is transformed into an angel of light.*

15. *Therefore it is no great thing if his ministers also be transformed as the ministers of righteousness; whose end shall be according to their works.* ***2 Corinthians 11:13-15***

- *If any man teach otherwise, and consent not to wholesome words, even the words of our Lord Jesus Christ, and to the doctrine which is according to godliness;* ***1 Timothy 6:3***

You are to contend for the faith as a true prophet, point people to the true Christian faith and correct and rebuke others who are teaching other doctrines.

- *As I besought thee to abide still at Ephesus, when I went into Macedonia, that thou mightest charge some that they teach no other doctrine,* ***1 Timothy 1:3***

It is your duty to make sure that false doctrine is not taught.

3. Because God Needs You

You are God's battle axe. You are the tool God will use in keeping the Christian faith in place. A workman is helpless and can do nothing without His work tools.

- *Thou art my battle axe and weapons of war: for with thee will I break in pieces the nations, and with thee will I destroy kingdoms*

Jeremiah 51:20

God needs you to contend for the faith.

4. Contend for the Faith Because You Will be Rewarded

"Behold, I am coming quickly,

- *But without faith it is impossible to please him: for he that cometh to God must believe that he is, and that he is a rewarder of them that diligently seek him.* **Hebrews 11:6**.

For the Son of man shall come in the glory of his Father with his angels; and then he shall reward every man according to his works.

Matthew 16:27

Contend for the faith because there is definitely a reward to your account. God is not a user of man; He is the rewarder of those who diligently seek him. therefore, faith is worth contending for.

Chapter Three
HOW DO I CONTEND FOR THE FAITH?

1. Have a Personal Relationship with God.

The first step to contending for the faith is to secure your salvation. Make sure you are saved. In Romans 10:9, *"That if thou shalt confess with thy mouth the Lord Jesus, and shalt believe in thine heart that God hath raised him from the dead, thou shalt be saved."* Once this is done, daily work is your salvation. Wherefore, my beloved, as ye have always obeyed, not as in my presence only, but now much more in my absence, work out your own salvation with fear and trembling.

Philippians 2:12.

Understand that Christianity is a relationship with Jesus; this means that Christ dwells in you. Having a personal relationship with God means walking with God, knowing

Him yourself, making Him have His place in your life as your God. It is only when the love of God is in our hearts that we can share it with others. You cannot fight a cause you do not care about, and you can never give what you don't have.

2. Translate These Christian Truths and Fundamental Doctrines to Everyday Experiences.

Imbibe and practice what the Christian faith teaches. Let it become a lifestyle. Let people see you and know that you are a Christian like the disciples of Jesus at Antioch.

For an unbeliever, praying in the name of Jesus, and getting results, can lead to conversion. Exhibiting the fruit of the Holy Spirit can convert another. You must learn to practice what the faith teaches and believes – both in secret and in the open – against any form of scrutiny or judgment, knowing that it is the truth.

The Bible says in Matthew 5:13-16,

13. *Ye are the salt of the earth: but if the salt have lost his savour, wherewith shall it be salted? it is thenceforth good for nothing, but to be cast out, and to be trodden under foot of men.*

14. *Ye are the light of the world. A city that is set on*

an hill cannot be hid.

15. Neither do men light a candle, and put it under a bushel, but on a candlestick; and it giveth light unto all that are in the house.

16. Let your light so shine before men, that they may see your good works, and glorify your Father which is in heaven. **Matthew 5:13-16**

You see, if you are not bold enough to practise these Christian truths, some lives will never get to glorify God and God will hold you responsible for your failure. Contend for this faith by consciously and systematically making sure that you live and operate within the confines of the Christian truth. There are bound to be oppositions; because the devil won't fold his hands and watch you prevail in victory as a living testimony of the gospel of Christ. He intends to keep believers in their old nature of sin and bondage, hence he sponsors affliction and storms into their lives so as to make them believe they are not yet liberated and give up on their new faith so he would lord over them.

That is why, no matter the contradictions you see as you walk with God, you should not give up but keep contending for the faith and the truth, which we proclaim will eventually swallow up the lies of the devil, just as the rod of Moses swallowed up the rod of the magicians. Light will forever prevail over darkness, so do not give up on that which you believe; contend for the faith in your marriage, family, business, ministry, academics etc. In every aspect of your life, you are to be a living testimony of the victory of Christ, which is total and complete victory over darkness. Your victory is the victory of that sister out there, it is the victory of that brother that is waiting to see your evidence and join you to serve your God.

Evidence silences argument. Each time there is an open show of light prevailing over darkness, the kingdom of darkness is depopulated, and the kingdom of light populated. That is why the devil can go to any length to fight a believer from shining forth. But as stated earlier, he is bound to fail when the believer holds on to the truth and contends for the faith.

- *...and this is the victory that overcometh the world, even our faith. 1 John 5:4.*

Abraham, the father of faith, who is the father of us all. For twenty-five years he kept hoping and believing God, until he became the father of many nations according to that which was spoken of him.

The Bible says of him:

19. *And being not weak in faith, he considered not*

his own body now dead, when he was about an hundred years old, neither yet the deadness of Sara's womb:

20.   *He staggered not at the promise of God through unbelief; but was strong in faith, giving glory to God;*

21.   *And being fully persuaded that, what he had promised, he was able also to perform.*

22.   *And therefore it was imputed to him for righteousness.* **Romans 4:19-22**

And in Genesis chapter 21, his evidence manifested.

1.   *And the LORD visited Sarah as he had said, and the LORD did unto Sarah as he had spoken.*

2.   *For Sarah conceived, and bare Abraham a son in his old age, at the set time of which God had spoken to him.*

3.   *And Abraham called the name of his son that was born unto him, whom Sarah bare to him, Isaac.*

4. *And Abraham circumcised his son Isaac being eight days old, as God had commanded him.*

5. *And Abraham was an hundred years old, when his son Isaac was born unto him.*

6. *And Sarah said, God hath made me to laugh, so that all that hear will laugh with me.*
Genesis 21:1-6

Beloved, Abraham contended for that which God said. He did not give in to the circumstances before him, he held on to that which God said and at the appointed time his testimony manifested. And Sarah said, "All that hear will laugh with me". In other words, everyone who hears my testimony will celebrate with me, they will align themselves with me, they will join me to glorify my God who changed my story to glory.

In Daniel chapter 3, the three Hebrew boys, Shedrach, Meshach, and Abednego, contended for the faith. They refused to bow down and worship the image that Nebuchadnezzar, the king, had set up; which was against the commandment of God. Report got back to the king and he called them and threatened to cast them into the midst of a burning fiery furnace if they 'fall not down and worship the image'. But right there and then, they declared their stand for the faith and absolute confidence in the God they serve, despite the burning fiery furnace being heated before them. So in anger, they were cast into the fire but to the glory of God, they were not burnt. Jehovah, who is a consuming fire, had gone ahead of them into the fire as the "fourth man". He had consumed and swallowed the potency of the physical fire and when they were cast in, the fire became a refreshing fire to them.

The Bible says,

- *And the house of Jacob shall be a fire, and the house of Joseph a flame, and the house of Esau for stubble, and they shall kindle in them, and devour them; and there shall not be any remaining of the house of Esau; for the LORD hath spoken it.* **Obadiah 18**

Our God, who is a consuming fire, will always show up strong for His children, who understand that they are fire and maintain their fire position, never compromising their faith in the midst of challenges or battles. And when He establishes the victory of such children, their obvious victory propels men to their faith. When the three Hebrew boys were not burnt and the king saw the fourth man with them in the fire, he made a decree.

29. *...That every people, nation, and language, which speak any thing amiss against the God of Shadrach, Meshach, and Abed-nego, shall be cut in pieces, and their houses shall be*

made a dunghill: because there is no other God that can deliver after this sort.

30. *Then the king promoted Shadrach, Meshach, and Abed-nego, in the province of Babylon.*
Daniel 3:29-30

Listen, when you contend for the faith in any issue of life, temporary discomfort and afflictions of life may arise, but when you stand firm in that which you believe, you will prevail gloriously, bringing praise and glory to God. That was the case of several who contended for the faith in scriptures, such as Daniel, who experienced the lion's den and came out unhurt. And the king made a decree that in every dominion of his kingdom, men should tremble and fear before the God of Daniel for He is the Living God... and Daniel prospered. (Daniel 6). Joseph, who flees from lying with Potiphar's wife, an act against his faith, and that landed him in prison but in due course God brought him out to the palace and promoted him in the land of Egypt.

Never compromise your faith or deny your identity, as some so-called Christians who do not want to be seen or identified as the born-again type do. Be bold to declare your identity. Let people know who you are.

I have gone out with a supposed Evangelist who met Muslims and declared that we were together; he meant Muslims and Christians are one because we serve the same God. An Evangelist who did not believe that Jesus is the only way according to scriptures in John 14:6. Believe and practice the Christian truth and doctrines.

3. Treat the Body of Christ as One

- *There is one body, and one Spirit, even as ye are called in one hope of your calling **Ephesians 4:4.***

- *So we, being many, are one body in Christ, and every one members one of another.*
  Romans 12:5.

- *Be kindly affectioned one to another with brotherly love; in honour preferring one another **Romans 12:10***

Scripture is clear about the body of Christ being one irrespective of its different parts.

- *For as the body is one, and hath many members, and all the members of that one body, being many, are one body: so also is Christ. **1 Corinthians 12:12***

Enough of denominational discrimination and segregation in the body of Christ. As individuals, let us begin to see and treat other Christians as our brothers and sisters in the faith.

So many founders of denominations have focused the eyes

of the people on themselves instead of pointing them to Jesus and have also made members believe that anyone who is not a member of their denomination is not on the right path.

4. *For while one saith, I am of Paul; and another, I am of Apollos; are ye not carnal?*

5. *Who then is Paul, and who is Apollos, but ministers by whom ye believed, even as the Lord gave to every man?* **1 Corinthians 3:4-5**

- *Is Christ divided? Was Paul crucified for you? Or were ye baptized in the name of Paul?* **1 Corinthians 1:13**

Beloved, there is a task in our hands as the church of Christ and only in unity as one body can we accomplish and complete this task. We must begin to learn to stand as one. Jesus Himself told us that;

- *And Jesus knew their thoughts, and said unto them, every kingdom divided against itself is brought to desolation; and every city or house divided against itself shall not stand:* **Matthew 12:25**

If we must win this contention against the Christian faith, unity of the church is the way to go. The body of Christ as we have seen in scriptures is one; we must not divide or separate by denominational differences or doctrines. Until some people witness the force of unity in the body of Christ, they will never see the Christian faith as one to be reckoned with.

The Christian faith is one bound by love; for God and fellow man. Matt. 22:37 & 39. "Charity they say begins at home". It is time for the church of God to build a formidable force against the world in which she exists, this can only be achievable by imbibing love as her culture. See every Christian as a fellow soldier in Christ, who is on the same mission, and join hands together in love at every opportunity to showcase Christ.

We must stop washing our dirty linen outside because of denominational differences. It does not matter the denomination, the fall of one Christian brother or sister to sin is not a call for castigation but a call for intercession because it is an attack on the entire church of Christ.

Do your best to keep the church as one in contention for the faith of the church.

4. Leave the Word of God the Way it is.

There are so many gimmicks and games in the body of Christ today that people are confused, not knowing what is truth anymore. To successfully contend for the faith, you must leave the word of God the way it is, just as God has instructed.

- *Ye shall not add unto the word which I command you, neither shall ye diminish ought from it, that ye may keep the commandments of the LORD your God which I command you.* **Deuteronomy 4:2**

- *What thing soever I command you, observe to do it: thou shalt not add thereto, nor diminish from it.* **Deuteronomy 12:32**

Inconsistency is not the nature of our God and no well-meaning person identifies with anything that is inconsistent. To win this battle, we must fight everything that stands against the word of God. Individuals, pastors and church founders must learn to put their fleshly desires aside and profess the word of God as it is.

Anyone who tampers with the word of God is incurring the wrath of God for trespassing and for misleading God's people.

18. *For I testify unto every man that heareth the words of the prophecy of this book, If any man shall add unto these things, God shall add unto him the plagues that are written in this book:*

19. *And if any man shall take away from the words of the book of this prophecy, God shall take away his part out of the book of life, and out of the holy city, and from the things which are written in this book.* **Revelation 22:18-19**

- *Whoever causes one of these little ones who believe in Me to sin, it would be better for him if a millstone were hung around his neck, and he were drowned in the depth of the sea.* **Matthew 18:6**

"For those who guide this people are leading them astray; And those who are guided by them are brought to confusion".

Do not tamper with God's word. If by this you mislead people, confuse them or hypnotize them for your own selfish gains, then you are not contending for the faith but against the faith. All must desist from making the word of God of no repute. Leave the word of God as it is, leave it as it instructs, and then you will be contributing somehow to keeping the fire and faith.

5. Study the Word of God

- *Study to shew thyself approved unto God, a workman that needeth not to be ashamed, rightly dividing the word of truth.* **2 Timothy 2:15.**

A workman must know his job and that includes his tools. It is the correct application of the tools that makes him a good workman. If he uses the wrong tools, he can never achieve success.

Every believer is a workman in the kingdom and his work tools are the word of God. You must therefore have a depth of knowledge of the word to be able to carry out your duties properly. The word of God teaches, guides, rebukes, encourages you, comforts, sustains and instils boldness and confidence in you as a good representative or ambassador of God's kingdom.

You must study to be an approved workman in the kingdom, both to be able to carry out your duties without hitches and to be able to apply the word. You are bound to make mistakes and be a bad example and teacher – like we have everywhere – if you do not know the word of God.

- *Jesus answered and said unto them, Ye do err, not knowing the scriptures, nor the power of God.* **Matthew 22:29**

To successfully contend for the faith, you must know scriptures. It is the only sure way to match the devil and be sure to defeat him. Jesus showed us an example of this.

You can only be assertive and definitive when you know scriptures, which is a function of study. To study:

- Deliberately set time aside to be with God. Find a time that will be convenient for you on daily basis.

- Prepare for your study; Bible, book, pen, concordance where available.

- Have a specific location of your study.

- Prepare your heart to talk to your Father, God. Equip yourself for the conversation.

6. Preach The Gospel

Contend for the faith by spreading it. This is the work of every believer. Our major work is to preach the gospel. It is not meant for only those on the pulpit but for everyone who enjoys the saving Grace of our Lord Jesus to joyfully invite others to know and enjoy the same Grace.

The devil is out there looking for whom to devour; *"Be sober, be vigilant; because your adversary the devil, as a roaring lion, walketh about, seeking whom he may devour."* 1 Peter 5:8. It is your duty as a child of God to show others the way to stay away from the devil's reach.

You are the witness of Christ and God's servant. According to Isaiah 43:10,

- *"Ye are my witnesses, saith the LORD, and my*

servant whom I have chosen: that ye may know and believe me, and understand that I am he: before me there was no God formed, neither shall there be after me." **Isaiah 43:10**

It is the duty of every Christian to contend for the posterity of our faith; this we must do by sharing our faith with others. The Apostles did not put an end to the work of Christ; you also must contribute, to hand it to other generations.

The Apostles contended for the Christian faith. They preached everywhere they went, they were dogged about it and over two thousand years later, people are still being saved. They contended for the faith and passed it on. You too must pass it on.

Somebody's salvation is tied to your preaching; someone's deliverance is waiting to manifest through you. Someone will receive healing and liberty thatwill in turn bring the person to the Christian faith. Do not bother yourself on how it will happen because you are not the doer; God is the doer and you only need to allow Him use you as an instrument.

8. *But what saith it? The word is nigh thee, even in thy mouth, and in thy heart: that is, the word of faith, which we preach;*

9. *That if thou shalt confess with thy mouth the*

Lord Jesus, and shalt believe in thine heart that God hath raised him from the dead, thou shalt be saved.

10. *For with the heart man believeth unto righteousness; and with the mouth confession is made unto salvation.*

11. *For the scripture saith, Whosoever believeth on him shall not be ashamed.*

12. *For there is no difference between the Jew and the Greek: for the same Lord over all is rich unto all that call upon him.*

13. *For whosoever shall call upon the name of the Lord shall be saved.*

14. *How then shall they call on him in whom they have not believed? and how shall they believe in him of whom they have not heard? and how shall they hear without a preacher?*
Romans 10:8-14

People need to be saved and if you do not preach, some will never get saved.

- *And he said unto them, Go ye into all the*

world, and preach the gospel to every creature. **Mark 16:15**

Preaching is the great commission of every child of God. Jesus has promised to be on our side when we go preaching the gospel.

18. *And Jesus came and spake unto them, saying, All power is given unto me in heaven and in earth.*

19. *Go ye therefore, and teach all nations, baptizing them in the name of the Father, and of the Son, and of the Holy Ghost:*

20. *Teaching them to observe all things whatsoever I have commanded you: and, lo, I am with you alway, even unto the end of the world. Amen.* **Matthew 28:18-20**

The kingdom of darkness is populated; we must contend for the faith to depopulate it by sharing our faith with others, to rescue the perishing.

- *Preach the word; be instant in season, out of season; reprove, rebuke, exhort with all longsuffering and doctrine.* **2 Timothy 4:2**

You must not be ashamed to preach the gospel, as this is

the excuse of so many people. You should be proud to let people know that you are saved.

- *For whosoever shall be ashamed of me and of my words, of him shall the Son of man be ashamed, when he shall come in his own glory, and in his Father's, and of the holy angels.* ***Luke 9:26***

8. *Also I say unto you, Whosoever shall confess me before men, him shall the Son of man also confess before the angels of God:*

9. *But he that denieth me before men shall be denied before the angels of God.* ***Luke 12:8-9***

After all your journey here on earth, it is better to be confessed before the Father and the angels than to be denied before them. Act wisely!

7. Pray

Contend for the faith in prayer. The place of prayer in the battle ground for our faith cannot be emphasised enough. Even Jesus engaged the force of prayer, and since He is the focus and standard for our Christian life, then it is right to say He set us an example to follow.

- *And in the morning, rising up a great while before day, he went out, and departed into a solitary place, and there prayed.* **Mark 1:35**

- *And he withdrew himself into the wilderness, and prayed.* **Luke 5:16**

Every battle in Christendom is sure to be won in the place of prayer. It is prayer that will supply Grace for you to do all that is required of you as a Christian. Hence, the importance of prayer.

Prayer is the only way we talk to God and receive instructions from Him. Therefore, the scope of prayer is not limited to certain issues.

- *But Jesus beheld them, and said unto them, With men this is impossible; but with God all things are possible.* **Matthew 19:26**

Nothing, therefore, should be seen as out of God's reach or too minute to bring before God. Scripture admonishes us to pray always; *"Praying always with all prayer and supplication in the Spirit, and watching thereunto with all perseverance and supplication for all saints."* **Eph. 6:18**.

- *I will therefore that men pray every where, lifting up holy hands, without wrath and doubting.* ***1 Timothy 2:8***

Prayer, as we see from the scripture above, is not time bound. Prayer does not really have to be dramatic before we know we are praying. You can make a simple sentence to God at your desk in the office, in the rest room, kitchen, car, board meeting, marketplace, talk to God right away and do a follow-up later. Pray always! Prayer has no time tag, irrespective of the issues you are presenting before God.

It is not an appointment with man that is bound by time and limited to location. Prayer is updating the ageless, timeless, tireless, weariless and boundless God.

Pray because your faith needs it to grow; "But ye, beloved, building up yourselves on your most holy faith, praying in the Holy Ghost." Jude 20. If your personal faith must grow from the point you gave your life to Jesus, you must learn to pray. If your faith must become a contending faith, you must pray.

Like we saw in Ephesians 6:28, all prayers must be done in the spirit. Anything not done in the Spirit in the kingdom to which we belong is noise, vain and a waste of time. God is a Spirit and you can only come to Him in the Spirit. If there is no network on your phone, your phone is totally useless; you cannot reach anybody nor can anyone reach you. So also is the spirit the connecting network that will make your call to heaven go through. Get connected to the spirit, be in the Spirit and get results.

- *God is a Spirit: and they that worship him*

must worship him in spirit and in truth.

John 4:24

Watching is part of praying. Why should you watch? You must to identify answers, obstacles, instructions, directions, and rebuke as the situation may warrant. This will determine the next line of action. You also need to watch to mark counter attacks for Holy Ghost demolition.

- *Watch ye and pray, lest ye enter into temptation. The spirit truly is ready, but the flesh is weak.* ***Mark 14:38***

Pray like Daniel, until you see your desire, don't stop (Daniel 10). The reason it seems you did not hear God well or that prophecy has not come to pass is because you allowed the Prince of Persia. You stopped praying.

Again, Ephesians 6:18 tells us to supplicate for the saints. Who are saints? All those active in the service of God: Pastors, Choristers, Ushers, Sanctuary keepers etc.: everyone who is redeemed by the blood of Jesus and is busy in God's house and in the service of God are saints who deserve intercession.

Praying for the saints is a sign that you care about God's people. It is showing God that you are interested in His business so that He can be interested in yours. It is contending for the faith.

The body of Christ needs prayers to break new grounds and reach new heights. Individuals in the church of God have issues that have refused to bow. The expiration of such issues is the salvation of another. You need to intercede. The truth is, if we know that when we pray on behalf of others, God answers and meets our needs faster, and we will engage the force of intercession.

INTERCEDING FOR SAINTS

- **Pray for Pastors and Missionaries**

- *And for me, that utterance may be given unto me, that I may open my mouth boldly, to make known the mystery of the gospel*
  Ephesians 6:19.

Pastors are humans; they need God to take over sometimes and they are at the forefront of the contention for the faith. They have a task to unravel the mystery of the gospel effectively and they need to do this with boldness.

1. *Finally, brethren, pray for us, that the word of the Lord may have free course, and be glorified, even as it is with you:*

2. *And that we may be delivered from unreasonable and wicked men: for all men*

*have not faith. **2 Thessalonians 3:1-2.***

- *Brethren, pray for us. **1 Thessalonians 5:25***

Pastors and missionaries need deliverance also. Pray that God will deliver them even as He gives them utterance from wicked and unreasonable men. They pray for you but they also have their own issues and are more exposed to attacks.

- **Pray Kingdom Advancement Prayers**

It is the responsibility of every believer to contend for the faith by praying that the kingdom of God will advance in length and breadth, word and power. Therefore pray!

1. *For Zion's sake will I not hold my peace, and for Jerusalem's sake I will not rest, until the righteousness thereof go forth as brightness, and the salvation thereof as a lamp that burneth.*

2. *And the Gentiles shall see thy righteousness, and all kings thy glory: and thou shalt be called by a new name, which the mouth of the LORD shall name.*

6. *I have set watchmen upon thy walls, O Jerusalem, which shall never hold their peace*

day nor night: ye that make mention of the LORD, keep not silence,

7. *And give him no rest, till he establish, and till he make Jerusalem a praise in the earth.*

Isaiah 62:1-2, 6-7

Every land needs God. Every land needs to be better and God has a purpose for each land. But for what we read from verse 1-2 to happen, verse 6-7 must be in place. For the kingdom of God to advance in your nation or environment, you must deliver yourself a watchman over the land; interceding day and night to make a change, without getting weary, until you see that change you desire.

Pray for the poor and the needy, the prisoners and everyone whose needs and challenges you can identify.

- *I exhort therefore, that, first of all, supplications, prayers, intercessions, and giving of thanks, be made for all men;* **1 Timothy 2:1**

- *And the LORD turned the captivity of Job, when he prayed for his friends: also the LORD gave Job twice as much as he had before.* **Job 42:10**

- *Bear ye one another's burdens, and so fulfil the law of Christ.* **Galatians 6:2**

- *Confess your faults one to another, and pray one for another, that ye may be healed. The effectual fervent prayer of a righteous man availeth much.* **James 5:16**

Child of God, imbibe intercession. Let it become your culture because;

- It is the will of God as seen in 1 Tim. 2:1

- It is the fulfilling of the law of Christ as in Gal. 6:2

- It has power embedded in it as seen in James 5:16.

God is still in the business of answering prayers and His words are ye and Amen. He will never relent on His promises to hear us when we pray.

- *The LORD is nigh unto all them that call upon him, to all that call upon him in truth.*

  Psalms 145:18

- *Then shall ye call upon me, and ye shall go and pray unto me, and I will hearken unto you.*

  Jeremiah 29:12

Chapter Four
CHARACTERISTICS OF CONTENDING FOR THE FAITH

Faith is an embodiment. Not all faith can contend. Your faith must get to the point where it can contend.

Your faith has to go from milk faith to meat faith and then to bone faith; children of God should grow from Grace to Grace.

- *But grow in grace, and in the knowledge of our Lord and Saviour Jesus Christ. To him be glory both now and for ever. Amen.*

    2 Peter 3:18

Trust

This is reliance on the integrity, strength, ability and surety of God. It is a belief in the reliability of God's abilities.

To successfully contend for the Christian faith, therefore, you need to have a firm belief in the reliability of God. Believe in the truth (the word of God) that you read. Rely on the integrity and strength of God to win the battle and live without an iota of doubt that He is able to win the battle.

5. Trust in the LORD with all thine heart; and lean not unto thine own understanding.

6. In all thy ways acknowledge him, and he shall direct thy paths.

7. Be not wise in thine own eyes: fear the LORD, and depart from evil. *Proverbs 3:5-7*

Rest in God's understanding, follow His plan and strategy, surrender to Him even in your thoughts. Look back on the times He came through for you, times He backed you up in defence of the faith, and just rest knowing that He is the same. The battle for the faith is actually the Lord's. You only need to yield yourselves as a vessel.

- *And he said, Hearken ye, all Judah, and ye inhabitants of Jerusalem, and thou king Jehoshaphat, Thus saith the LORD unto you, Be not afraid nor dismayed by reason of this great multitude; for the battle is not yours, but God's.* **2 Chronicles 20:15**

Obedience

Obedience is an offshoot of trust; when you trust a person enough, you obey with ease. Trust cannot be complete without obedience. Your obedience must be complete for your faith to contend properly. In the kingdom, there is no room for partial obedience because it amounts to complete disobedience. For your faith to win this battle, understand that it is not about you, but God. So trust him enough to obey all of His instructions and follow through His methods.

Jesus showed us an example of obedience to the point of His death for us on the cross.

- *And being found in fashion as a man, he humbled himself, and became obedient unto death, even the death of the cross.* **Philippians 2:8**

You can only appreciate this work of Christ's obedience on the cross by complete obedience to Him. It is a sign of love for God to walk in obedience.

- *If ye love me, keep my commandments.* **John 14:15**

- *Jesus answered and said unto him, If a man love me, he will keep my words: and my Father will love him, and we will come unto him, and make our abode with him. John 14:23*

Obedience is to hear God's word and act on it accordingly. Obedience to God's command is the true sign of love for God. It's also a sure way to get God's blessings.

- *But he said, Yea rather, blessed are they that hear the word of God, and keep it.* **Luke 11:28**

- *And this is love, that we walk after his commandments. This is the commandment, That, as ye have heard from the beginning, ye should walk in it.* **2 John 1:6**

Sacrifice

Total trust and obedience in and to God requires a great deal of sacrifice, as it will always interfere with your desires, beliefs, hopes. It will interfere with your understanding and methods.

- *For whosoever will save his life shall lose it: but whosoever will lose his life for my sake, the same shall save it.* **Luke 9:24**

- *I beseech you therefore, brethren, by the mercies of God, that ye present your bodies a living sacrifice, holy, acceptable unto God, which is your reasonable service.* **Romans 12:1**.

Contend for the faith by being a living sacrifice. Sacrifice is giving up something that you want to keep, especially in order to get or do something else. Sacrifice is an act of offering to God something precious. The most precious thing you have to offer is your life. Give it to God as a living sacrifice and it will be easy to give up anything in response or obedience to God.

Get to the point where your faith can contend in victory in these dimensions of "trust", "obedience", and "sacrifice".

The necessity of contending for the faith is laid upon us as truth keepers of the word of God. Remember, the people of sodom had no Bible, and our God has no grandchild. Please don't forget that the Christian race is personal. And That is Why we have been encouraged to contend for the faith earnestly, honestly. Seriously and sincerely.

If the angels who kept not their proper position were punished despite being creatures who saw God face to face, how do you think we as mortal beings can escape if we neglect God's great salvation?

Also, remember the Israelites after crossing the red sea, mark you, none of them died in Egypt instead on their way to the promised land.

To contend for the faith, we have to have the faith of God, see things from the perspective of the eyes of God, just the same way Joshua and Caleb who went out to spy, while others saw giants and failure, they were full of faith and saw their enemies as grasshoppers because they were faithful in faith

– Rev Samuel Madu Osunwa

A sister I know contended for the faith despite her Barbaric kindred law, and God showed up for her.

During the early 80's, in Amafor Umuaka in Imo State Nigeria, a new law was enacted that anyone who attended Assemblies of God church Umuaka would pay the sum of 100 Naira. While some people adhered to the law, one sister contended for her faith and continued attendance to the church. Unfortunately, the next time she went to the church, she got beaten and her Bible torn by the son of a powerful native doctor in Amafor Umuaka Imo State.

She wept bitterly and told the boy that God would tear him just like he tore her Bible. Just as the sister proclaimed, the boy became disabled and could not go back to school. All efforts his father made to get him healed proved abortive. This incident led to the abolition of the barbaric law as the fear of God gripped everyone in the village. And brought freedom to all Christians in Amafor to serve God without restrictions in the Assemblies of God church Umuaka.

The Lord also used this incident to save me from being rapped by a man 1 bumped into while walking home at night after visiting my brother in Nnewi, Anambra State. When the man wanted to rape me, the Lord gave me wisdom, and l threatened him that my God would make him disabled like he did to the other man. He got scared and ran away.

I ascribe all Glory to the Almighty God for his supernatural intervention.

As believers, we are to ensure that the standard of our faith is not lowered no matter what. We are called to abstain from wrong doctrine and immoral lifestyles that might endanger our faith and bring the name of our God into disrepute.

We as Christians are called to contend with all the weapons at our
   disposal in Ephesians 6:13-18.

We are to let our manner of life be worthy of the gospel of Christ" (Phil. 1:27).

We are to watch and pray and be watchmen for the truth and cannot simply watch in silence as people slip into error. Ezekiel 3:16 - 21.

Remember, as a Christian, others may live as they like, but you cannot.

-Veronica Chinasa Osunwa

Conclusion

Rise up to take your place on the battle ground for the Christian faith. Brace yourself up as one of the labourers for the harvest of this end time for indeed ...*The harvest truly is plenteous, but the labourers are few. **Matthew 9:37**.*

Find your place in the house of God and serve tirelessly. Take your everyday ordinary life and place it in God's hand and see how He turns it around for purposeful living. God is not interested in your ability but in your availability.

Bring yourself to the point that you know God and His word such that you cannot be swayed. Only then can you contend firmly unto victory for the faith.

14. *That we henceforth be no more children, tossed to and fro, and carried about with every*

wind of doctrine, by the sleight of men, and cunning craftiness, whereby they lie in wait to deceive;

15. *But speaking the truth in love, may grow up into him in all things, which is the head, even Christ:*

16. *From whom the whole body fitly joined together and compacted by that which every joint supplieth, according to the effectual working in the measure of every part, maketh increase of the body unto the edifying of itself in love.*

17. *This I say therefore, and testify in the Lord, that ye henceforth walk not as other Gentiles walk, in the vanity of their mind,*

18. *Having the understanding darkened, being alienated from the life of God through the ignorance that is in them, because of the blindness of their heart:*

19. *Who being past feeling have given themselves over unto lasciviousness, to work all uncleanness with greediness.*

20. *But ye have not so learned Christ;*

21. *If so be that ye have heard him, and have been taught by him, as the truth is in Jesus:*

22. *That ye put off concerning the former conversation the old man, which is corrupt according to the deceitful lusts;*

23. *And be renewed in the spirit of your mind;*

24. *And that ye put on the new man, which after God is created in righteousness and true holiness.*

25. *Wherefore putting away lying, speak every man truth with his neighbour: for we are members one of another.*

26. *Be ye angry, and sin not: let not the sun go down upon your wrath:*

27. *Neither give place to the devil.*

28. *Let him that stole steal no more: but rather let him labour, working with his hands the thing which is good, that he may have to give to him that needeth.*

29. Let no corrupt communication proceed out of your mouth, but that which is good to the use of edifying, that it may minister grace unto the hearers.

30. And grieve not the holy Spirit of God, whereby ye are sealed unto the day of redemption.

31. Let all bitterness, and wrath, and anger, and clamour, and evil speaking, be put away from you, with all malice:

32. And be ye kind one to another, tender-hearted, forgiving one another, even as God for Christ's sake hath forgiven you. **Ephesians 4:14-32***.*

www.ingramcontent.com/pod-product-compliance
Lightning Source LLC
Chambersburg PA
CBHW020330010526
44107CB00054B/2062